D1465754

CHINA FOCUS

ANCIENT CHINA

Edited by Charlotte Guillain

Heinemann Library
Chicago, Illinois

© 2008 Heinemann Library
a division of Pearson Inc., Chicago, Illinois

Customer Service   888–454–2279

Visit our website at www.heinemannlibrary.com

Designed by Richard Parker and Manhattan Design
Printed by China Translation Printing Services

12 11 19 09 08
10 9 8 7 6 5 4 3 2 1

Library of Congress Cataloging-in-Publication Data
Guillain, Charlotte.
  Ancient China / Charlotte Guillain. -- 1st ed.
      p. cm. -- (China Focus)
  Includes bibliographical references and index.
  ISBN-13: 978-1-4329-1216-1 (hc)
  1. China--History--Juvenile literature. I. Title.
  DS735.G95 2008
  931--dc22
                              2007049475

Acknowledgments
The publishers would like to thank the following for permission to reproduce photographs: ©akg-images pp. **10–11**, **15** (Laurent Lecat), **19**, **22**; ©Ancient Art & Architecture Ltd (Dr. S. Coyne) p. **12**; ©The Art Archive pp. **14** (Bibliotheque Nationale Paris), **18** (The British Library), **23** (Musee Cernuschi Paris/Dagli Orti), **26** (Freer Gallery of Art), **27** (British Museum), **30** (National Palace Museum Taiwan); ©Bridgeman Art Library pp. **8** (Museum of Fine Arts, Houston, Texas, USA), **17** (Bibliotheque des Arts Decoratifs, Paris, France, Archives Charmet), **25** (Bibliotheque des Arts Decoratifs, Paris, France, Archives Charmet), **29** (Bibliotheque des Arts Decoratifs, Paris, France, Archives Charmet), **34** (Bibliotheque Nationale, Paris), **35** (Oriental Museum, Durham University, UK), **37** (Arthur M. Sackler Museum, Harvard University Art Museums, USA, Bequest of Grenville L. Winthrop), **39** (Museumslandschaft Hessen Kassel); ©Corbis pp. **4** (Zefa/Fridmar Damm), **9** (Lowell Georgia), **13** (Free Agents Limited), **33** (Royal Ontario Museum), **38** (Asian Art & Archaeology, Inc.); ©Natural History Museum p. **6**; ©Science & Society Picture Library p. **24**; ©Smithsonian, Freer Art Gallery, Washington DC p. **41**; ©TopFoto (Alinari 2006) p. **21**; ©Werner Forman Archive pp. **28** (Beijing Museum), **32** (Idemitsu Museum of Art, Tokyo).

Cover photograph of the terracotta army, Shaanxi Province, China, reproduced with permission of ©Getty Images.

The publishers would like to thank Jane Shuter, Clare Hibbert, Ali Brownlie Bojang, Melanie Guile, Dale Anderson, Jameson Anderson, Cath Senker, and Neil Morris for additional material.

Every effort has been made to contact copyright holders of any material reproduced in this book. Any omissions will be rectified in subsequent printings if notice is given to the publisher.

Contents

Some words are printed in bold, **like this**. You can find out what they mean by looking in the glossary.

Amazing and Ancient!

China is a huge country in Asia, about 5.9 million square miles (9.5 million square kilometers). It is so big that different areas of China have very different climates. These regions range from cold, dry deserts to hot, humid rain forests. People first started to settle in China in river valleys with rich soil that was good for farming.

The Chinese **civilization** began more than 5,000 years ago. It is one of the oldest civilizations in the world today. The ancient Chinese had many new ideas in science, art, and other fields of learning. Their inventions include paper, math, and fireworks.

Many other countries also took on Chinese **culture**, adding Chinese beliefs and practices to their own ways of life. This book covers the time from the earliest settlements in China and explores the amazing stories, beliefs, art, inventions, and discoveries that ancient China has given us.

The landscape in China varies greatly. Parts of the countryside are famous for their beauty.

Legend

- Xia Kingdom
- Shang Kingdom
- Qin Kingdom
- Modern China

N
W — E
S

RUSSIA

KAZAKSTAN

MONGOLIA

KYRGYZSTAN

KOREA

CHINA

Dunhang

Anyang

Xian

Erlitou

NEPAL

BHUTAN

INDIA

BANGLADESH

MYANMAR
(BURMA)

LAOS

VIETNAM

0 ——— 500 miles
0 ——— 1000 km

This map shows modern China and three of the early kingdoms of ancient China.

Clans to Kingdoms

People first lived in China about 700,000 years ago. After living in caves, they hunted and then farmed along the Huang He ("hwong heh") River. Between 10,000 and 5,000 BCE people started to create small villages of about 300 people living in 50 to 100 houses. These people lived in large family groups, called **clans**. Small villages of up to 50 houses usually had only one clan. Bigger villages had two or three clans.

The early Chinese farmed, fished, and kept animals. Some villages were built with earth walls around them. **Archeologists** think that the villagers started to fight each other, trying to take more land. A wall around the village would have protected the people who lived there when they were attacked.

Archeologists have found the bones of people who lived between 500,000 and 250,000 years ago. This picture shows what the whole skull of a person named "Beijing Man" looked like.

Dynasties

Kings and emperors started to rule different parts of ancient China. They were organized into **dynasties**. Most dynasties were made up of powerful families. These families joined together with other families in the area. They agreed to help protect each other against enemies.

China's Dynasties

During its long history, China was ruled by several dynasties. Early on, different families ruled in different parts of the country, so some of them were powerful at the same time as other dynasties. Later on, only one dynasty at a time ruled the whole country.

c.1600–1050 BCE	Shang Dynasty
c.1050–256 BCE	Zhou ("joh") Dynasty
221–206 BCE	Qin ("chin") Dynasty
206 BCE–220 CE	Han Dynasty
220–589 CE	Six dynasties period
581–618 CE	Sui ("sway") Dynasty
618–907 CE	Tang ("tahng") Dynasty
907–960 CE	Five dynasties period
960–1279 CE	Song ("soong") Dynasty
1279–1368 CE	Yuan ("yoo-en") Dynasty
1368–1644 CE	Ming Dynasty
1644–1911 CE	Qing ("ching") Dynasty

The Xia Dynasty

For years, no one has been sure whether the Xia Dynasty existed. Chinese **myths** and stories exist about the Xia, but there is no written evidence. In 1959, archeologists found objects that may be from the Xia Dynasty.

Some historians believe the Xia Dynasty might have ruled part of China before 1600 BCE. Some think the Xia were farmers who used **bronze** weapons. They also may have made pottery and prayed to spirits to help them.

The Shang Dynasty c. 1600–1050 BCE

The Shang Dynasty became powerful after the Xia. Shang rulers controlled a large area of northeastern China from about 1600 to 1050 BCE.

The Shang used several **technologies** to conquer more lands. Bronze weapons helped them take land from people who still used stone weapons. The Shang also used **chariots**, giving their armies extra speed and power.

Another important technology was to use writing. The Shang were not the first Chinese people to use writing, but they made the writing system much better.

Religious leaders

Shang Dynasty rulers also were **religious** leaders. The Shang people believed that their kings could talk to their **ancestors**. They worshipped the Shang Di, a god whom they believed controlled other gods, such as the gods of the sun, moon, wind, and rain.

The Shang bronze workers were far more skilled than any other bronze workers in the world at that time.

Royal tombs

Shang rulers showed their power by building special **tombs**. They made thousands of people dig huge holes in the ground and build large burial rooms out of wood. Other workers spent months creating the pottery, **jade**, bronze, and other objects that went into the tombs.

About 30 kings ruled throughout the Shang Dynasty. Myths tell that the last king, Di Xin, did not take care of his people well. The stories say he took money from them and did not protect them. He lost control and was defeated by the Zhou Dynasty.

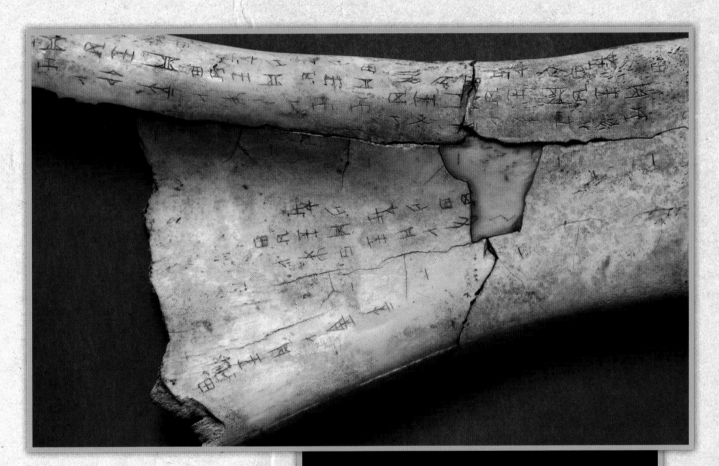

This bone has writing from the Shang Dynasty on it.

Oracle bones

To speak to their ancestors, Shang rulers used oracle bones. These were animal bones, often from an ox or part of a turtle shell. When the king asked his ancestor a question, a priest pressed a hot poker into a spot on the bone. The answer—yes or no—depended on how the bone cracked. On many of these bones, the priest wrote down the question and then the answer.

The Zhou Dynasty c.1050–256 BCE

Shang armies often fought against neighboring peoples, such as the Zhou who lived in a kingdom to the west. Eventually a Zhou king conquered the Shang in about 1050 BCE. Zhou kings then led the most powerful **state** in northern China for the next few hundred years.

A new dynasty

The Zhou set out to capture more land in China, and their kingdom grew to be much larger than the Shang kingdom.

The Zhou ruled in a way that became very important to Chinese civilization. They worshipped the god called Heaven, and the Zhou king was praised as the "son of Heaven." The Zhou claimed that Heaven only allowed a king to rule as long as he was good to his people. If he did not rule well, Heaven would take the kingdom from him.

Changing society

The Zhou rulers gave large gifts of land to their families and to trusted **officials**. The people who received these gifts were in charge of thousands of **peasants**. When the landowners and officials died, the land and peasants were passed on to their sons.

In this society, the king was at the top. Beneath him were the landowners. Next came the officials who ran the government or managed the **nobles'** lands. At the bottom were the farmers. This system stayed in place in China for thousands of years.

Break up of the dynasty

The Zhou Dynasty lasted 794 years, from c.1050–c. 256 BCE. During the last part of the Zhou Dynasty, the rulers lost control. This time is known as the "Warring States Period," because of a series of wars between different Chinese states. Despite the wars, this was a great time for **philosophers**. Ideas such as **Confucianism**, **Daoism**, and **Legalism** are from this time (see pages 34–35). Some of the most famous Chinese poetry also was written at this time.

Bronze bells like these were popular in Zhou times. They were often placed in the tombs of wealthy lords.

The Chinese Empire

The Qin Dynasty 221–206 BCE

The Qin used military skill, **bribery**, and spying to conquer the other kingdoms and create China's first **empire** in 221 BCE. Their leader, Zheng, renamed himself as Qin Shi Huangdi ("she hwong dee"), the First **Emperor** of Qin. He believed that China needed a new start.

The First Emperor

The First Emperor made people throughout his empire use the same writing, the same coins, and the same weights and measures in the markets. He even made them make carts the same size to fit the new roads that were being built all over the empire. This made transportation and communication much better. He did not respect **scholars** and banned the teachings of the thinker Confucius, because he taught respect for age, experience, and the past. Government officials were sent throughout the emperor's lands to make sure that his new laws were obeyed.

This is a terracotta statue of the First Emperor, Qin Shi Huangdi.

The early Great Wall was built of earth and pebbles. It was also built of reeds and wood. Over time the earth was replaced with stone.

Great Wall

The Great Wall of China was first built in sections by small states that wanted to defend themselves. As new rulers took power, the walls were rebuilt and made longer. The First Emperor ordered that the walls be connected to make one great wall that curved about 4,500 miles (7,300 kilometers) from east to west across northern China. Along the wall were watchtowers where the emperor's men watched for enemies.

So many people died building the Great Wall from accidents and attacks by robbers that it has been called "the longest graveyard in the world."

GREAT WALL FACTS

- Length: 4,500 miles (7,300 kilometers)
- Workers: criminals and farmers
- Deaths among workers: about 1 death for every 5 feet (1.5 meters) of wall
- Additional workers: elephants may have done some of the heavy lifting

A new way of ruling

The First Emperor wanted control of his empire. So he took lands from nobles and made them move to his capital city, Xianyang. He divided China into 36 areas. Each area had a military leader, someone to run day-to-day life, and an inspector who checked up on the others and reported to the First Emperor. These officials collected **taxes**, checked markets, and punished criminals. Only men could become officials. They had to pass a set of tests that were held every few years.

Under the First Emperor, there were many laws. The punishments for breaking them were tough. If people were caught with certain books, they could be executed or sent to work on the Great Wall until they dropped dead from exhaustion. But cities and farmland were not being destroyed by war anymore. There was peace. The emperor always reminded people of this if he thought they would not like a new law.

NO TALKING

Only an emperor's family, nobles, and important officials could talk directly to him.

This painting shows the First Emperor punishing scholars.

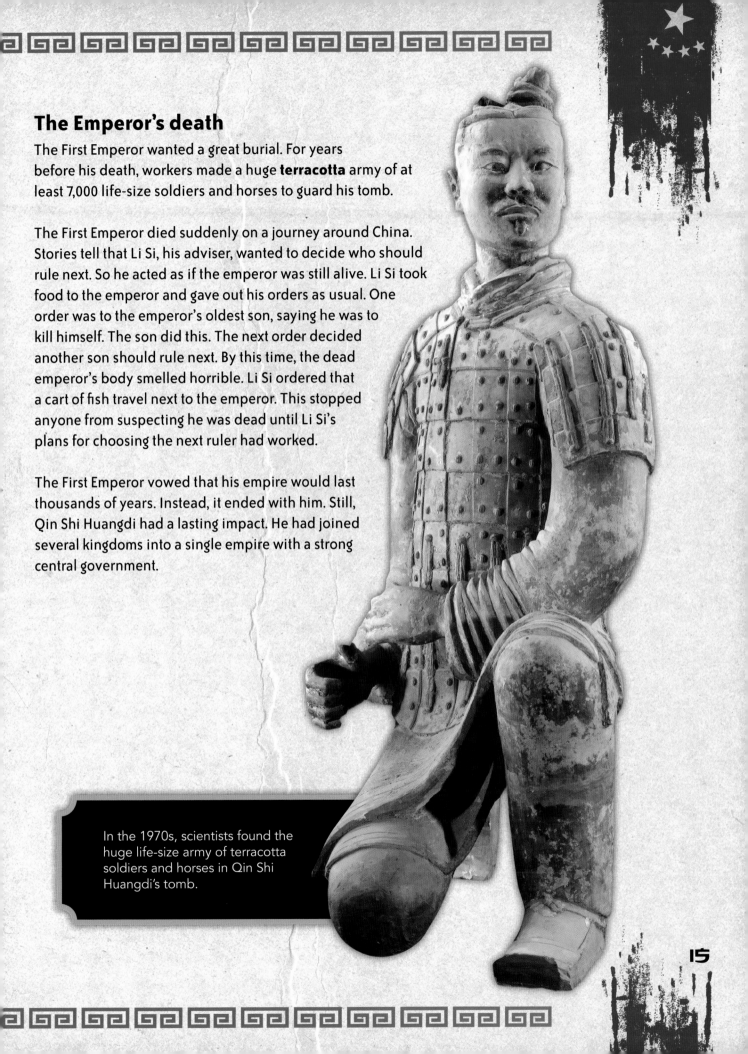

The Emperor's death

The First Emperor wanted a great burial. For years before his death, workers made a huge **terracotta** army of at least 7,000 life-size soldiers and horses to guard his tomb.

The First Emperor died suddenly on a journey around China. Stories tell that Li Si, his adviser, wanted to decide who should rule next. So he acted as if the emperor was still alive. Li Si took food to the emperor and gave out his orders as usual. One order was to the emperor's oldest son, saying he was to kill himself. The son did this. The next order decided another son should rule next. By this time, the dead emperor's body smelled horrible. Li Si ordered that a cart of fish travel next to the emperor. This stopped anyone from suspecting he was dead until Li Si's plans for choosing the next ruler had worked.

The First Emperor vowed that his empire would last thousands of years. Instead, it ended with him. Still, Qin Shi Huangdi had a lasting impact. He had joined several kingdoms into a single empire with a strong central government.

In the 1970s, scientists found the huge life-size army of terracotta soldiers and horses in Qin Shi Huangdi's tomb.

The Han Dynasty

After Qin Shi Huangdi died, wars broke out across northern China as different leaders tried to take control from the new emperor. The victor was Xiang Yu, who was helped by a man called Liu Bang. Liu Bang had been born a peasant and worked for the government in Qin times. Xiang Yu gave Liu Bang control of a region of western China as a reward for his help. Liu soon revolted against Xiang Yu and in 206 BCE he became emperor himself and took the name Gaozu ("gao-zoo").

Gaozu's **reign** started the Han Dynasty, which ruled China for the next 400 years. This period was generally peaceful and successful. Han emperors began a system of **imperial** government that later dynasties followed. This meant that there was strong central control of an empire that included many different groups of people. The Han Dynasty was the first to have a full-time army of trained soldiers. The government welcomed advice from scholars and **Buddhism** came to China from India during the Han Dynasty.

HAN RULE

Han rule was so important in Chinese history that even today Chinese people call themselves "children of the Han."

Troubled empire

Still, historians think that Han rule was not all happy and peaceful. This might be because Han emperors had many wives and many sons. Struggles for power may have occurred when powerful sons—and their powerful mothers—refused to accept the **heir** named by the emperor. Children gaining the throne at a young age caused another problem. **Regents** ruled until these children became adults. Some regents were not always willing to give up power when the young emperor was old enough to rule himself.

This silk painting from the 1600s CE shows how an artist imagined Emperor Wudi leaving his palace.

Han China often was attacked by **nomads** from Central Asia and Mongolia. Emperor Wudi, who reigned from 141 to 87 BCE, continued work on the Great Wall of China to defend his empire. Wudi's structure was not simply a wall. It was defended at all times by soldiers. Every few miles or so, there was a watchtower, and every 18 miles (30 kilometers) there was a fort.

Changing dynasties

In 581 CE, General Yang Jian established the Sui Dynasty, which lasted until 618 CE. The Sui emperors made the Great Wall stronger and constructed a series of canals. Millions of men were forced to work on these two projects. The people rebelled and the Tang Dynasty was set up in its place.

The Tang Dynasty

During the Tang Dynasty a new banking system was introduced. Buddhism became very popular, supported by China's first and only empress, Wu Zetian (625−705 CE). She was a brilliant but **ruthless** ruler, who murdered her rivals to become Emperor Gaozong's favorite. When the emperor became ill in 660 CE, Wu Zetian took over the government and declared herself Empress.

The Song Dynasty

At the end of the Tang Dynasty, there was another time of chaos, known as the Five Dynasties. But in 960 CE, the Song Dynasty brought a large part of the country together again. This was a time of great new steps in map-making, mathematics, engineering, and astronomy.

Wu Zetian ruled successfully during one of ancient China's most peaceful periods.

CRIME AND PUNISHMENT

The Mongols had terrible punishments for crime. Stories tell us that robbers were beaten with a cane up to 100 times and many died of their wounds. Anyone who was caught stealing a horse was cut in two by a sword.

Mongol rule

In 1206 CE the **Mongol** leader, Genghis Khan (c. 1162-1227 CE), led his army toward China. He defeated China and it became part of a huge Mongol empire.

In 1279 CE, the new leader, Genghis Khan's grandson Kublai Khan (1215–94 CE), set up a Mongol dynasty of emperors, the Yuan. They ruled China for almost a century. China's Mongol rulers started **trade** between east and west again because they controlled all the land on the trade routes. Foreigners began arriving in China, including the European trader Marco Polo (see pages 22–23).

The Ming Dynasty

By 1368 CE, the Ming Dynasty had driven the Mongols from China. The Ming Dynasty (1368–1644 CE) is famous for producing beautiful pots and vases, but also is remembered for being very powerful and sometimes very cruel toward the peasants.

This silk painting shows Genghis Khan out hunting.

Trade and Invention

In Han times, the Chinese began to have more contact with the outside world. Chinese culture spread to the lands we now call Korea and Vietnam. For China, however, the most important link was with Central Asia, which was crossed by the Silk Road.

The Silk Road

The Silk Road was a route that connected China to the **Middle East** and Europe through deserts and mountains. Many goods were traded along the way. From China there were herbal medicines, silk, pottery, paper, and gunpowder. Gold, grapes, and rugs came from the west. The Great Wall helped to protect traders who traveled along this route.

New ideas

Ideas also traveled along the Silk Road. The religion of Buddhism came to China from India along this route. Chinese inventions, from silk-making to ironworking were carried to the west.

The Silk Road was not just one road, but a series of trade routes that went from stopping place to stopping place.

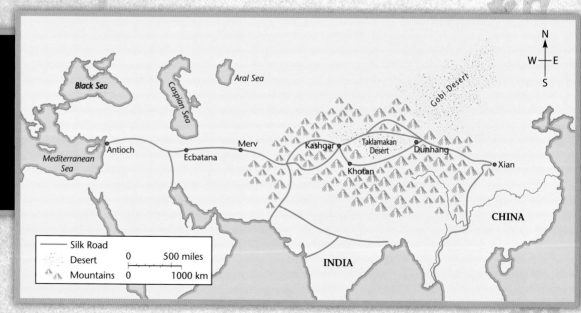

Black Sea

Caspian Sea

Aral Sea

Gobi Desert

Mediterranean Sea

Antioch

Ecbatana

Merv

Kashgar

Taklamakan Desert

Khotan

Dunhang

Xian

CHINA

INDIA

N
W E
S

— Silk Road
Desert
Mountains

0   500 miles
0   1000 km

The Pamir Mountains form a huge barrier to travel in Central Asia. It is incredible that the Polos survived the climb over them.

Marco Polo

Marco Polo (c. 1254–1324 CE) was born in Italy. In 1271 he traveled east with his father, Niccolo, and uncle, Maffeo, perhaps to bring back silks to sell in the city of Venice. Around 1274, they reached a place called Kashgar on the Silk Road. Most travelers from the West stopped here to sell goods, but the Polos carried on. In early spring 1275, during the Song Dynasty, the Polos crossed the Taklamakan Desert. After 30 days in the desert, the Polos arrived in Dunhuang on the borders of China. Worn out, they rested for a while and traded with the Tibetan Buddhists. In May 1275, after walking for many more days, the Polos reached Kublai Khan's palace at Shangdu. Their journey had taken three and a half years. The emperor Kublai Khan accepted their gifts and had a feast prepared. Marco was amazed at the fabulous palace, with its decorations and its beautiful lake and gardens.

MUSK

As he was traveling toward Kublai Khan's palace, Marco smelled musk, a perfume, in the air. It came from the musk ox, an animal similar to an antelope but the size of a goat. He described how the locals killed a musk ox and used parts of its stomach, which they dried to make the perfume.

Marco and the Mongols

After their long journey, the Polos settled down in China, moving to the winter palace in Beijing with Kublai Khan. Maffeo and Niccolo probably continued as merchants. Marco quickly took on Mongol **customs** and managed to learn four new languages.

The Polos saw that Kublai Khan ruled a well-ordered society. Marco discovered useful inventions not known in Europe. The Mongols used paper money, which was much easier to carry around than gold or silver coins. They also had a postal service. Messengers carried important letters on horseback, and could cover an incredible 250 miles (400 kilometers) in one day. Marco found "a sort of black stone which burns … and gives out much more heat than wood." This was coal. It was known in Europe but not used very much at the time.

WATCH YOURSELVES

Marco Polo described how the Mongols sometimes fought. "Now and then they pretend to flee, shooting arrows backwards, so killing as many men and horses as if they were fighting face to face!"

Kublai Khan traveled in great style, here in a luxury tent carried by elephants.

This porcelain plate, beautifully decorated with a fish and a flower, was made in China just before the time of Marco Polo.

Marco's mission

Kublai Khan liked Marco and loved hearing about his travels. The emperor asked Marco to travel around the Mongol Empire as his spy.

Traveling through China, Marco saw amazing sights. The streets of Hangzhou in eastern China all were paved with stone or brick. In Europe, most streets were dirt tracks. A dam had been built to redirect the river and prevent it from flooding the city. The city even had a fire department!

In Hangzhou, beautiful cups, plates, and bowls were made from **porcelain**. Nobody knew yet how to make this fine pottery in Europe. Elsewhere in China, Marco saw how silk was produced.

When he returned to Venice, Marco wrote down his adventures. His book, *The Travels of Marco Polo*, was a mixture of information about people and places he had seen with his own eyes, other travelers' stories, and fantastic tales that he had heard.

Inventions and discoveries

Many important inventions came from ancient China. These include useful things such as paper and printing, the umbrella, the **abacus**, the wheelbarrow, canals, and the magnetic compass.

Paper

Before the invention of paper, the ancient Chinese either wrote on silk or on bamboo strips. They needed something that was cheaper and tougher than these materials. First, they experimented with paper made from the hemp plant. This was very thick. Mixing the hemp with bark and rags made a thinner paper.

The wheelbarrow

Stories from ancient China tell of a man who built himself "a wooden goat or sheep" to carry things in around 100 BCE. A Han tomb has a carving on the wall that shows a man pushing a wheelbarrow.

NOODLES

The ancient Chinese were eating pasta before the Italians. Noodles are made in the same way as Italian pasta.

The magnetic compass was the first really safe way to work out direction when people were at sea, out of sight of land.

Gunpowder also was used to make fireworks. This painting shows fireworks being used as part of a celebration. Kites are flying in the background.

Warfare

Other inventions include items that made the ancient Chinese stronger in war, such as gunpowder and steel for sharper swords. Kites were used in wartime to send messages to prisoners. Sometimes they were made to create strange sounds and flown over the enemy to distract them.

The rudder

A rudder is like a long oar that is fixed to the back of a ship to help steer it. Archeologists have found several models of ships in Han tombs that have rudders. The ancient Chinese were well ahead of the West in boat design.

Chinese knowledge

The Chinese also studied the stars and planets and they invented ways of keeping time. Chinese medicine, especially **acupuncture**, is used by many people all over the world today. The Chinese also worked out how to move water for farming and how to predict earthquakes.

Daily Life

Farming

Most ancient Chinese people lived and worked in the countryside. They grew a variety of crops, depending on where they lived. In the north they grew grain, such as wheat and **millet**. In the south where it was wetter, farmers grew rice. Most people grew vegetables and kept chickens and pigs. Most farming was done with hand tools. Some richer farmers could afford to use oxen plows and carts.

In spring, the emperor was the first to plow a field. This showed that farming was very important. But even though farmers were important to the empire, they usually were the poorest people.

This painting shows families collecting rice by hand, watched by an official.

THE COUNTRYSIDE

These lines are from an ancient Chinese poem about the countryside:

The peace of the countryside

"Floating on the river are shining insects,
The reeds and grasses on the banks reflect in the water.
My heart feels peaceful and calm
The slow clear stream is pleasing."

This pottery model of part of a farm was made during the Han Dynasty.

CHINESE FARMERS

Farmers worked hard throughout the year. Chao Cuo ("chah-oh coo-oh"), wrote in 178 BCE that, "They labor at plowing in the spring and **hoeing** in the summer, harvesting in the autumn and storing foodstuff in winter."

Farmers' lives

In Han times, the government taught farmers to keep the soil healthy by planting different crops each year. Many waste products, including human waste, were spread on the fields to **fertilize** the crops.

Hard work

As well as working on their farms, and doing a period of military service, all men had to work for the government one month each year. Farmers were used to build palaces and tombs and help with government industries.

Most families could just manage to live off their crops. However, the emperors made farmers pay taxes. For many farmers, their daily work, forced labor, and taxes were simply too much. Many gave up their own land and worked for large landowners so they could be paid a regular wage. In Han times, farmers paid lower taxes because the government wanted to help them.

Towns and industry

The first cities were important places for government and religion. In Zhou times, cities grew larger and also became centers of industry and trade. New emperors often had a new city specially built for them. These cities were carefully planned, with the emperor's palace and the government offices surrounded by his relatives and officials.

Cities were surrounded by walls made of earth to protect them. Many cities had big marketplaces and special streets set aside for different businesses. Smaller towns grew bit by bit. They had many wooden houses on narrow, twisting streets. These houses could catch fire and burn down very easily.

People who lived in ancient Chinese cities often worked and traded in the markets.

This illustration shows the traditional methods used to make paper from bamboo. Papermaking became an important industry in ancient China.

Life in cities

Life in the cities was exciting. People filled the streets to buy and sell, and street entertainers performed for the crowds. However, the ancient Chinese thought farmers were more important than the different groups of city people, despite their poverty. Ancient China was divided into four groups: scholars and officials were seen as most important, followed by farmers. Next came craft workers and, at the bottom, merchants. Laws were made to stop merchants from wearing silk and riding in carriages. They also were not allowed to own land or become officials. These laws were not always kept, but they show how hard life could be for merchants.

Growing industries

Many new industries grew up in imperial times. The Chinese first began using iron during the Zhou Dynasty. During the Warring States Period, iron makers became rich. The Han government stopped them from getting too powerful by taking over the iron trade. It also took control of the salt industry and the grain trade.

Family life

To the ancient Chinese, family was more special than friends or business. The most important member of a family was the oldest man. Everyone had to obey him, even his adult sons. In return, he was expected to look after the rest of the family, from his oldest son to the least-important servant. He had to give them a home, clothes, and food, and he had to educate his children.

Separate lives

Although the family was so important to ancient Chinese life, families in rich and important **households** actually spent very little time together. They had large homes, with separate living areas for women. The women of the family stayed at home, while the men spent much of their work and free time away from the home. Poorer families mixed together more. In farming villages, a family lived in one room. But even in these villages, the men spent most of their work and free time together, away from the women.

This picture shows an adult son and his wife and children greeting his parents. The wife is bringing them breakfast. Children were expected to value and obey their parents all their lives.

The emperor and his **nobles** wore richly decorated silk robes. The robes were too long to run or work in. This showed that whoever wore these robes did not work.

Farmers wore clothes made from cheap fabric. These clothes were comfortable to work in.

Scholars and their wives wore less-expensive clothes. But their robes were long, and their shoes had curled toes. They were hard to work or run in.

Clothes

Wealthy people wore long **robes** made from expensive silk fabrics that were decorated beautifully. There were rules about what colors people could wear. There were special colors for the emperor. From around 1000 CE until the 1900s, rich women had their feet bound. Their feet were wrapped tightly in cloth from birth. This broke the bones and made the feet like tiny stumps. Many people thought the way these women walked looked beautiful, but it was very painful.

Poor people wore pants and shorter jackets that were practical to work in. They wore flat shoes or went barefoot.

Food

Rich people in ancient China ate a huge amount of meat. Vegetables were seen as food for people who could not afford meat. On special occasions, they ate unusual meats, such as snakes and carefully prepared small birds. Everyday meats included pork, chicken, lamb, goose, and duck. Poor people ate vegetables and either rice or porridge made of millet, barley, or oats. They did not eat meat very often.

Entertainment

While peasants spent most of their time working, rich people enjoyed music, dancing, theater, and games.

Music and dancing

The ancient Chinese were very interested in music. In fact, they wrote the words "music" and "enjoyment" in the same way. The Han government even created an official whose job was to collect traditional and folk songs.

Dancing happened during festivals. Dancing also was used to celebrate the New Year or the emperor's birthday. Many religious **ceremonies** involved dancing. Groups of dancers toured from village to village to perform.

Other entertainment

Acrobats did balancing acts, such as walking on tightropes, and other tricks. Puppet masters used puppets to act out stories. In shadow puppet shows, an entertainer shone light behind wooden figures shaped like people. This made shadows on a background.

MUSICAL INSTRUMENTS

Ancient Chinese musicians played many different musical instruments. They grouped their instruments by the material they were made from, such as silk, bamboo, wood, clay, and animal skin.

This model of a musician was put in the tomb of an important person.

These pottery figures are playing the gambling game called *liubo*.

Games

The Chinese enjoyed games. One popular game, called *yi* ("yee"), was an early version of a modern Japanese game known as *go*. In this game, players moved small pieces on a square board with criss-crossing squares. A gambling game called *liubo* ("lee-oo-boh") also was popular.

Sports

The ancient Chinese often played a game similar to soccer. Noble men and women also played a version of polo on horseback. These versions of soccer and polo both were used as training exercises for the army.

The most common sport was hunting. The ancient Chinese trained birds to hunt. Nobles and peasants both hunted for rabbits and pheasants. Nobles also enjoyed archery and **fencing**.

CHINESE SPORTS

Other sports that some historians think the ancient Chinese invented:

- Golf, known as *chiuwan*. It had tees, holes in the ground marked with a flag and a stick, and golf clubs with bamboo handles and hard wooden heads.
- Badminton, which was played by two people who hit a "bird" (a feathered shuttlecock) to each other, trying to keep it in the air.

Traditions and Beliefs

Philosophers told people what the world means and how people should react to the world. Confucianism, Daoism, and Legalism were the three main schools of **philosophy** to emerge from the Zhou Dynasty.

Confucianism

Confucius was born in 551 BCE. He served a local king, but when he felt that his advice was not followed, he left and began teaching. He believed that everyone should be happy with where they are in life. Confucius said that everyone is born good and has a duty to take care of each other.

Confucius thought the family was very important in society. Fathers had the responsibility of raising and caring for their children. It was important to show respect for parents and ancestors.

TWO SAYINGS OF CONFUCIUS

- "The ruler of a large state must be trust worthy, not wasteful of resources, and care for the people."

- "A man who behaves well to his parents and shows kindness to others doesn't upset those above him."

In this painting, Confucius is carrying the five Confucian texts that scholars had to learn.

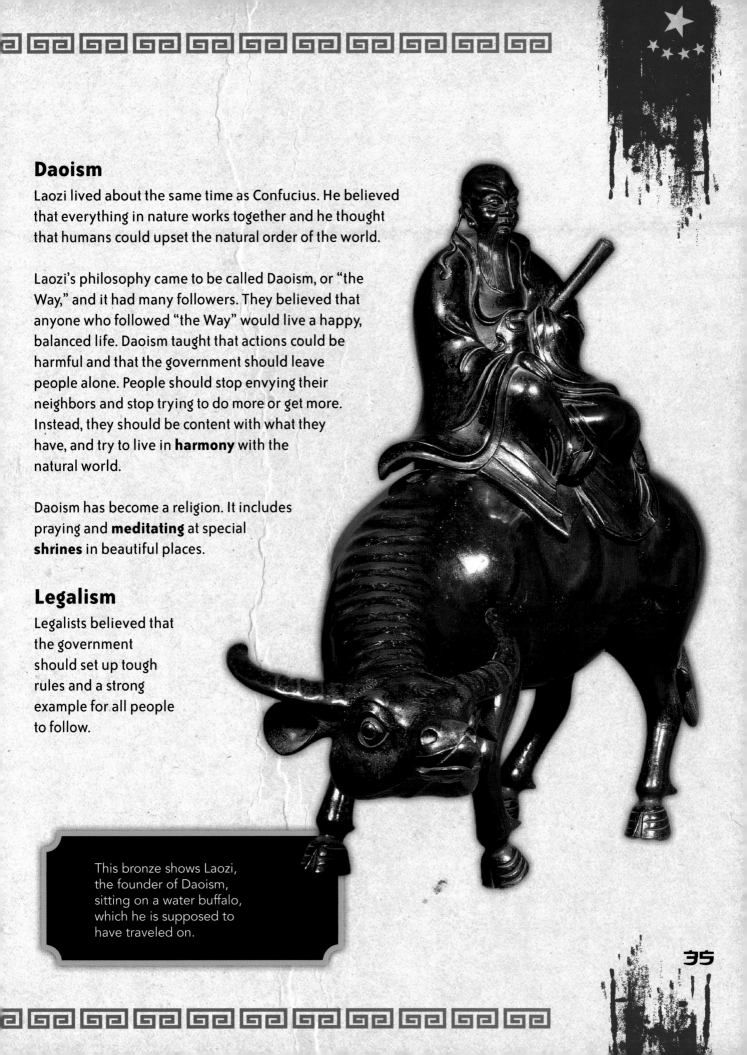

Daoism

Laozi lived about the same time as Confucius. He believed that everything in nature works together and he thought that humans could upset the natural order of the world.

Laozi's philosophy came to be called Daoism, or "the Way," and it had many followers. They believed that anyone who followed "the Way" would live a happy, balanced life. Daoism taught that actions could be harmful and that the government should leave people alone. People should stop envying their neighbors and stop trying to do more or get more. Instead, they should be content with what they have, and try to live in **harmony** with the natural world.

Daoism has become a religion. It includes praying and **meditating** at special **shrines** in beautiful places.

Legalism

Legalists believed that the government should set up tough rules and a strong example for all people to follow.

This bronze shows Laozi, the founder of Daoism, sitting on a water buffalo, which he is supposed to have traveled on.

Traditional beliefs

The ancient Chinese believed that a number of gods, goddesses, and spirits affected their everyday life. Nature spirits were thought to have come to Earth either as spirits or as ordinary people. They could bring rain, good luck, or even toothache! Spirits existed for different parts of life, such as wealth, health, children, and happiness. All these spirits had to be kept happy.

The Queen Mother

In Han times people believed in a mountain spirit called the Queen Mother of the West. Daoists believed that she was the ruler of an **immortal** kingdom. The Queen Mother of the West was joined by another figure, the King Father of the East. This balance of west and east reflected the idea of *yin* and *yang*, which required balance in all things. A blessing from Han times read: "May you attain the highest political rank like the King Father of the East. May you attain longevity like the Queen Mother of the West."

The ancient Chinese believed in "yin," the female force, which was balanced by "yang," the male force.

BE PATIENT!

The ancient Chinese thought that losing your temper was extremely rude. Good behavior was so important that laws were made about it.

Ancestors

From Han times, people had great respect for their ancestors. They believed that the spirits of the dead went to an **afterlife** that was just like ordinary life. These spirits were thought to have power over life on Earth. So the ancient Chinese looked after family tombs carefully, leaving offerings for dead family members. They also prayed to them. They believed their ancestors could help them or—if the ancestors were unhappy—make life difficult.

Buddhism

During the Han Dynasty, (206 BCE–220 CE) a new religion reached China from India, brought by travelers along the Silk Road (see page 20). This religion was Buddhism and it became very popular. Buddhists practiced meditation. They believed in behaving well to each other, and in **reincarnation** after death.

Buddhism became especially popular during the difficult times toward the end of Han rule and following the fall of the Han Dynasty. In the next few centuries, more and more Chinese people became Buddhists. By around 500 CE, China had more than 10,000 Buddhist temples and nearly 160,000 Buddhist monks.

This is a bronze statue of the Buddha.

Burials

Like the ancient Egyptians, the ancient Chinese believed in life after death. From Han times they filled the tombs of their rulers with many goods to ensure that they had everything they needed in the next life. Even ordinary people were buried with possessions to help them after death.

Preserving bodies

The Chinese never developed the skill in **preserving** dead bodies that the ancient Egyptians had. Still, they tried hard to protect the dead. Jade symbolized eternal life and was thought to give protection from evil spirits and decay. For these reasons, jade objects were placed with bodies from early times. Later, amazing burial suits were made. Some members of the Han imperial family are buried in suits made of tiny jade plates. The bodies have since decayed, but archeologists have reconstructed the suits to show how they originally fitted.

This burial suit was for a princess who died in the 2nd century BCE.

Burial attendants

The tombs of Shang rulers and nobles contain the skeletons of servants who were buried alive so they could look after their master's spirit after death. A tomb from around 1200 BCE included 90 servants and several animals. Some Shang burials contained entire chariots, along with the horses needed to pull them.

Burial attendants still were buried in Zhou times, but there were not so many. The First Emperor of Qin's tomb is known for the thousands of terracotta soldiers and other attendants, but it also contained the skeletons of officials and servants. In later times, small figures made of pottery, jade, wood, and metal were placed in tombs instead of people.

Huge tombs

The tomb of the First Emperor of Qin was a huge complex covering 20 square miles (52 square kilometers). The central burial mound is supposed to have looked like a miniature version of the world, with parts shaped like mountains and valleys. Han tomb builders carved their tombs out of rock, making caves. One tomb resembles a home, and even includes a bathroom.

This painting shows a funeral procession.

The End of Imperial China

In the 1600s, the Ming Dynasty was replaced by the Qing Dynasty. The first Qing emperors were foreigners who only managed to hold onto power because of their strong army. They made some tough laws and even forced all Chinese men to wear their hair in a pigtail!

Later, Qing emperors (1644–1912 CE) defeated their enemies and ruled well so that life became peaceful for many Chinese people. However, during this time, more and more European traders were coming to China. The emperors were worried these foreigners would try to take land from China. Many Chinese people were smoking the drug **opium** at this time and the British became the main traders in opium. This led to a war between Britain and China that ended in Britain taking Hong Kong from China and gaining trading rights in five ports.

More European countries started to take control in other parts of China. Many Chinese people rebelled against this and millions of people died. The last emperor, Pu-Yi, was only three years old when he became emperor. He only reigned for four years, because in 1911 imperial rule came to an end. For many of the years that followed, China was torn apart by wars and social change. The once-proud empire was destroyed.

THE LAST EMPEROR
Pu-Yi was allowed to live in the palace of the Imperial City after 1911. He was given a payment of around $4.8 million a year. In 1924 he was sent away from the palace. When he died in 1967 he was working as a gardener.

Despite its difficult ending, the Chinese empire always will be remembered for its beautiful arts and crafts, its inventions and discoveries, its colorful characters, its brilliant ideas and philosophies, and its amazing stories. The ancient Chinese influenced people all around the world for many centuries and their knowledge and ideas continue to affect our lives today.

This painting shows farmers in ancient China irrigating a field. It was important to be able to find water for farming.

Timeline

c. 8000 BCE
Farming begins in China.

2000 BCE
Chinese learn to make bronze.

1600–1050 BCE
Shang Dynasty, the first dynasty to leave historical records, rules northern China.

1200 BCE
Shang Dynasty adopts chariots from Central Asia.

Shang rulers begin using oracle bones to answer questions.

About 1050 BCE
Zhou king overthrows Shang and establishes Zhou Dynasty.

551–479 BCE
These are the dates when historians think Confucius lived.

500s BCE
This is the period when historians think Laozi lived.

400s BCE
Metal coins come into use in China.

403–221 BCE
There is prolonged fighting between competing rulers, called the Warring States Period.

300s BCE
The *Laozi*, one of the basic books of Daoism, is written down.

221 BCE
Qin Shi Huangdi becomes First Emperor of China.

210 BCE
Qin Shi Huangdi dies and fighting breaks out.

206 BCE
Gaozu becomes emperor, launching Han Dynasty.

141–87 BCE
Emperor Wudi, who expanded China, rules.

111 BCE
Government takes over production of iron, salt, and alcohol.

Han rule has extended by this time to parts of present-day Korea and Northern Vietnam.

1 CE
Chang'an, the Han capital, has a population of nearly 250,000.

2 CE
Population of Han China is 58 million.

9–23 CE
Wang Mang interrupts Han rule but is overthrown.

25 CE
Emperor Guang Wudi restores Han Dynasty.

90–125 CE
Han rule enjoys last period of great power and prosperity.

105 CE
This is the traditional date the Chinese give for the invention of paper.

220 CE
The Han Dynasty ends.

220–589 CE
During this time different parts of China are ruled by six dynasties, and it is not united.

538/539 CE
Trade with the west via the Silk Road allows Westerners to appreciate Chinese art.

581–618 CE
The Sui Dynasty rules China.

c. 600 CE
Porcelain production is perfected in China.

618–907 CE
The Tang Dynasty rules China.

907–960 CE
Five Dynasties—during this time, different parts of China are ruled by different dynasties, and it is not united.

960–1279 CE
The Song Dynasty rules China.

c. 1000 CE
Paper is first used as a painting surface.

1279 CE
Mongols from the north take over ancient China. They settle and create their own dynasty, the Yuan.

1368–1644 CE
Ming Dynasty rules China.

1644–1911 CE
Qing Dynasty rules China.

Glossary

abacus device that uses beads to help add, subtract, multiply, and divide

acupuncture medical treatment in which needles are put into the body at certain points to cure illnesses

afterlife where some people believe you go when you die

ancestor someone who lived before you in your family, like a grandparent

archeologist person who studies the past by looking at monuments and artifacts from certain cultures

bribery giving people money and things so they will do what you want

bronze metal that is a mixture of copper and tin

Buddhism religion based on the teachings of the Buddha

ceremony special actions performed at important occasions

chariot wheeled carriage pulled by a horse in battle

civilization society with a high level of art, science, and government

clan large group of families who are related to each other

Confucianism teachings of the thinker Confucius

culture actions and beliefs of a society

custom usual way of behaving in a certain situation

Daoism religion based on the ideas of Laozi combined with the ideas of Buddha

dynasty families who rule an area for more than one generation

emperor ruler who has total power, like a king

empire all the lands controlled by one country

fencing fighting with swords

fertilize add substances to soil to help crops grow

harmony state of agreement

heir person who inherits money, property or power

hoe loosen soil with a special tool

household everyone living in the same house; the family and their servants

immortal thing that lives forever

imperial to do with the emperor

jade hard, bluish-green precious stone

Legalism tough belief system that the First Emperor of Qin followed

meditation calming the mind by focusing attention on something simple, such as breathing or an image

merchant person who buys and sells goods

Middle East countries between the Mediterranean Sea and Iran

millet wheat-like grain, used for making bread and beer

Mongol person from Mongolia, a country that was next to China

myth traditional tale

noble important person

nomad person who moves around from place to place following a food supply

official person working for the government

opium drug made from poppies

peasant farm worker

philosopher someone who studies the purpose of life

philosophy way of thinking about the world

porcelain type of pottery that can be baked at a high temperature until very hard and smooth

preserve stop something, for example a body, from decaying

regent adult who rules a kingdom or empire in the name of a child ruler

reign length of time that a king or queen rules

reincarnation coming back to life on Earth as a different person, animal, or thing

religious involved in a system of belief or worship

robes long, flowing clothes

ruthless pitiless or merciless

scholar someone who studies a particular subject

shrine special place to worship

state country or part of a country

tax fee paid to a ruler or government

technology scientific knowledge used in practical ways

terracotta baked clay

tomb place where dead people are buried

trade buy and sell goods

Further Information

Books

Anderson, Dale. *Ancient China*. Chicago: Raintree, 2005.

Anderson, Jameson. *The History and Activities of Ancient China*.
    Chicago: Heinemann Library, 2007.

Immell, Myra. *The Han Dynasty*. Chicago: Lucent Books, 2002.

Sherman, Josepha. *Your Travel Guide to Ancient China*.
    Minneapolis: Lerner Publications, 2003.

Places to visit

Many museums have good Chinese collections. Here are some of the more
famous ones:

The Metropolitan Museum of Art
1000 5th Ave at 82nd Street
New York, NY 10028-0198
(212) 535-7710 www.metmuseum.org

The Art Institute of Chicago
111 South Michigan Ave
Chicago, IL 60603
(312) 443-3600 www.artic.edu

Asian Art Museum of San Francisco
200 Larkin Street
San Francisco, CA 94102
(415) 581-3500 www.asianart.org

Websites

China Knowledge
www.chinaknowledge.de
This site has a wide variety of information on history, art, and culture.

National Gallery of Art – The Golden Age of Chinese Archaeology
www.nga.gov/education/chinatp_toc.htm
This site displays and discusses many ancient Chinese objects, from prehistoric times to the Qin and Han dynasties, found in recent decades.

Metropolitan Museum of Art – The Timeline of Art History
www.metmuseum.org/toah/splash.htm
At this Metropolitan Museum of Art site, you can see and read about Chinese artifacts from different times in ancient China by choosing the time period and then East Asia.

British Museum – Terracotta Army Exhibition
www.thefirstemperor.org.uk/
At this British Museum site you can learn about the First Emperor and his terracotta army.

Index